Connect

SECOND EDITION

Workbook 2

CAMBRIDGE
UNIVERSITY PRESS

CAMBRIDGE
UNIVERSITY PRESS

University Printing House, Cambridge CB2 8BS, United Kingdom

One Liberty Plaza, 20th Floor, New York, NY 10006, USA

477 Williamstown Road, Port Melbourne, VIC 3207, Australia

4843/24, 2nd Floor, Ansari Road, Daryaganj, Delhi – 110002, India

79 Anson Road, #06–04/06, Singapore 079906

Cambridge University Press is part of the University of Cambridge.

It furthers the University's mission by disseminating knowledge in the pursuit of education, learning and research at the highest international levels of excellence.

www.cambridge.org
Information on this title: www.cambridge.org/9780521737074

First published 2004
Second edition 2009
40 39 38 37 36 35 34 33 32 31 30 29 28 27 26 25 24 23

Printed in Dubai by Oriental Press

A catalogue record for this publication is available from the British Library

ISBN 978-0-521-73703-6 Student's Book 2 (English)
ISBN 978-0-521-73704-3 Student's Book 2 (Portuguese)
ISBN 978-0-521-73707-4 Workbook 2 (English)
ISBN 978-0-521-73708-1 Workbook 2 (Portuguese)
ISBN 978-0-521-73709-8 Teacher's Edition 2 (English)
ISBN 978-0-521-73710-4 Teacher's Edition 2 (Portuguese)
ISBN 978-0-521-73706-7 Class Audio CDs

Art direction, photo research, and layout services: A+ comunicação
Book design: Adventure House, NYC

Table of Contents

New friends

1 **Complete the questions. Then answer the questions.**

1. *Where* are you from?
   I'm from Brazil.

2. _____ old is your best friend?
   _____

3. _____ your birthday?
   _____

4. _____ Rio de Janeiro in Mexico?
   _____

5. _____ you on the soccer team?
   _____

6. _____ Tokyo?
   _____

7. _____ your name?
   _____

8. _____ your best friend from?
   _____

2 **Write questions and answers.**

1. **Q:** (where / San Francisco) *Where's San Francisco?*
   A: (California) *It's in California.*

2. **Q:** (who / they) _____
   A: (my / classmates) _____

3. **Q:** (how / old / Angelo) _____
   A: (13) _____

4. **Q:** (you / in / Sabrina's class) _____
   A: (yes) _____

5. **Q:** (your / name) _____
   A: (Nina) _____

6. **Q:** (who / she) _____
   A: (my science teacher) _____

Neighborhoods

1 Complete the conversation with the words in the box.

☐ are there any ☐ there are ☐ there aren't ☐ there isn't
☑ is there a ☐ there are no ☐ there is a ☐ there's no

Beth Hi, Tasha. What's your new school like?

Tasha Well, it's not very big, but it's nice.

Beth *Is there a* swimming pool?

Tasha No, _____ . But _____ swimming pool in my neighborhood.

Beth _____ tennis courts?

Tasha Yes, _____ . _____ basketball courts, though. That's OK, because I can't play basketball!

Beth Where's the mall? Is it near your school?

Tasha _____ mall near my school. _____ any stores near my school.

Beth Too bad!

2 Write questions. Then answer the questions with information about your neighborhood.

1. **Q:** (parks) *Are there any parks?*
   A: *Yes, there are.*

2. **Q:** (big library) _____
   A: _____

3. **Q:** (movie theater) _____
   A: _____

4. **Q:** (tennis courts) _____
   A: _____

5. **Q:** (shoe stores) _____
   A: _____

6. **Q:** (gym) _____
   A: _____

7. **Q:** (restaurants) _____
   A: _____

8. **Q:** (skating rink) _____
   A: _____

1 Complete the questions. Then match the questions to the correct answers.

1. _Who_ are they ? _____   a. No, there isn't.

2. _____ there a library in your neighborhood? _____   b. They're my brothers.

3. _____ your name? _____   c. No, she's not.

4. _____ your birthday? _____   d. Yes, there are.

5. _____ there any baseball fields at your school? _____   e. It's in July.

6. _____ she from Puerto Rico? _____   f. I'm from Venezuela.

7. _____ are you from? _____   g. I'm 14.

8. _____ old are you? _____   h. My name's Hector.

2 Answer the questions.

1. **Q:** Is there a skating rink in the park?
   A: (yes) _Yes, there is._

2. **Q:** How old is Barry?
   A: (12 / not 13) _____

3. **Q:** When's your birthday?
   A: (December / not May) _____

4. **Q:** Is there a gym in your school?
   A: (no) _____

5. **Q:** Are you in Mrs. Giavatto's history class?
   A: (no / Mr. Valli) _____

6. **Q:** Who are they?
   A: (not my teachers / my parents) _____

1 Number the sentences in the correct order.

_____ Wow! He's good at tennis.

_____ And who's that?

_____ Yes, he's really athletic. He's also pretty good at soccer and baseball.

_____ That's Rico's friend, Steve.

_1_ Hi, Brian. Who's that?

_____ He's not good at tennis.

_____ Hello, Jenna. That's my friend, Rico.

_____ You're right. But he can tell great jokes. He's funny.

2 Complete the sentences with the words in the box.

☐ artistic ☐ draw ☐ funny ☑ musical
☐ athletic ☐ friendly ☐ languages ☐ smart

1. She can play a lot of instruments.
   She's _musical_ .

2. He can make friends easily.
   He's _____ .

3. She's good at drawing.
   She's _____ .

4. She can tell great jokes.
   She's really _____ .

5. He's good at soccer and volleyball.
   He's _____ .

6. She's good at math, computers, and English.
   She's _____ .

7. He can speak four _____ .

8. I can _____ great pictures.

3 Write sentences with *good at, pretty good at,* and *not good at* about people you know.

1. (English) _Lisa's not good at English._

2. (painting) _____

3. (music) _____

4. (science) _____

5. (math) _____

6. (sports) _____

Lesson 4 — Our pets

1 Choose the correct words to complete the conversations.

1. **A** Snakes are cool. I like snakes _a lot_ (a little / a lot).

   B Not me. I don't like snakes _____ (a lot / at all).

2. **A** I don't like parrots _____ (a little / very much).

   B Really? Parrots are active. I like parrots _____ (a lot / at all).

3. **A** Spiders are dangerous. I don't like spiders _____ (a little / at all).

   B Spiders are OK. I like spiders _____ (a little / a lot).

4. **A** Cats are boring and messy. I don't like cats _____ (a lot / very much).

   B Oh, cats aren't bad. I like cats _____ (very much / a little).

2 Match the pictures to the correct conversations in Part 1. Write the correct numbers in the boxes.

a 4

b

c

d

3 What do you think of these animals and things? Do you like them? Write sentences with your own information.

1. (cats) _Cats are cute. I like cats a lot._

2. (music stores) _____

3. (concerts) _____

4. (dogs) _____

5. (video games) _____

6. (comic books) _____

7. (computers) _____

8. (parrots) _____

Get Connected
UNIT 1

1 Read the Web site quickly. What can Nora do?

_____

www.coolanimals.gc/

Animals with Talent

Can animals think? Are they artistic? Are they musical? Here are two stories about animals with special talents:

In Thailand, there's a group of very interesting elephants. These elephants are good at drawing. They can also paint. Their pictures are beautiful and interesting.

People look at the pictures and say, "These elephants are really artistic and smart." You can see the pictures in special stores and on the Internet.

Nora is a beautiful gray cat, but she isn't a typical cat. She can play the piano! Nora's owner, Betsy, is a music teacher. There are two pianos in Betsy's living room. Nora plays both. Nora likes the pianos a lot. She likes to play the piano with Betsy's students. Her music is very nice.

Nora is friendly – and famous, too. There's a video about Nora on the Internet, and she has a Web site. There are articles about Nora in newspapers, too.

Are there any amazing animals in your town?

2 Check (✓) the correct words to complete the sentences.

1. My sister can draw and paint. She's   ☑ artistic.   ☐ friendly.

2. Cecile can play the piano. She's   ☐ athletic.   ☐ musical.

3. Tommy can speak four languages. That's not   ☐ typical.   ☐ special.

4. Angelina Jolie is an actress. Many people love her. She's   ☐ famous.   ☐ musical.

5. My brother gets good grades in school. He's   ☐ beautiful.   ☐ smart.

3 Read the Web site in Part 1 slowly. Answer the questions.

1. Where are the elephants from? _They're from Thailand._

2. Are the elephants good at drawing? _____

3. Where can you see the pictures? _____

4. Is Betsy an English teacher? _____

5. Is there a video about Nora? _____

A Complete the conversations with the sentences in the box.

> ☐ Are you in Mrs. Cook's class? ☐ She's 12. ☑ Where are you from?
> ☐ It's in October. ☐ What's your name? ☐ Who are they?

1. **A** *Where are you from?*
   B I'm from Los Angeles.
2. **A** _____
   B My name's Regina.
3. **A** How old is she?
   B _____

4. **A** _____
   B They're my classmates.
5. **A** When's your birthday?
   B _____
6. **A** _____
   B No, I'm not.

B Complete the questions with *Is there a* or *Are there any*. Then look at the pictures, and answer the questions.

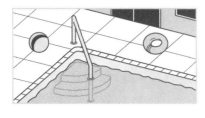  

1. **Q:** *Is there a* swimming pool?
   A: *Yes, there is.*

2. **Q:** _____ restaurants?
   A: _____

3. **Q:** _____ mall?
   A: _____

4. **Q:** _____ tennis courts?
   A: _____

5. **Q:** _____ gym?
   A: _____

6. **Q:** _____ movie theater?
   A: _____

C Write sentences with *like* or *don't like*.

1. (I / dogs / a little) *I like dogs a little.*
2. (I / rabbits / a lot) _____
3. (I / cats / at all) _____
4. (I / spiders / very much) _____
5. (I / snakes / at all) _____
6. (I / parrots / a lot) _____

School days

1 Complete the sentences about Esteban's day with the words in the box.

☐ do homework   ☐ eat breakfast   ☐ eat dinner   ☑ get up   ☐ go to bed   ☐ go to school

1. Every day, I *get up* at 7:00.

2. At 7:45, I _____ with my family.

3. I _____ with my friends.

4. After school, I _____ .

5. I _____ with my sister.

6. I _____ at 10:00.

2 Write sentences.   👍 = things I do   👎 = things I don't do

1. get up / 7:00 👍 / 8:00 👎

   I get up at 7:00. I don't get up at 8:00.

2. eat breakfast / with my friends 👎 / with my family 👍

   _____

3. eat lunch / cafeteria 👍 / home 👎

   _____

4. do my homework / school 👎 / home 👍

   _____

5. watch TV / with my friends 👍 / with my teachers 👎

   _____

6. go to bed / 10:30 👍 / 11:30 👎

   _____

Free time

1 **Complete the conversations with the words in the box**
and *Do you*, *Yes, I do*, or *No, I don't*.

☑ collect	☐ listen	☐ take	☐ watch
☐ hang out	☐ play	☐ talk	☐ write

1. **A** *Do you collect* _____ trading cards?

   B *Yes, I do.* _____ I collect baseball trading cards.

2. **A** _____ sports?

   B _____ I'm not very athletic.

3. **A** _____ at the mall after school?

   B _____ I go home after school.

4. **A** _____ to music?

   B _____ My favorite singer is Shakira.

5. **A** _____ music lessons?

   B _____ I take piano lessons.

6. **A** _____ DVDs?

   B _____ DVDs are boring.

7. **A** _____ e-mail messages?

   B _____ I write e-mail messages every day.

8. **A** _____ on the phone?

   B _____ I talk on the phone with my friends every day.

2 **Complete the questions with the words in the box. Then match the questions**
to the answers.

☐ collect	☐ hang out	☐ play	☐ take
☑ draw	☐ listen to	☐ play with	☐ use

1. Do you *draw* pictures? *h*
2. Do you _____ the Internet? ____
3. Do you _____ soccer? ____
4. Do you _____ at the mall? ____
5. Do you _____ music? ____
6. Do you _____ dance lessons? ____
7. Do you _____ stamps? ____
8. Do you _____ your dog? ____

a. Yes, I do. I'm pretty good at sports.
b. No, I don't. I hang out at the library.
c. Yes, I do. They're very interesting.
d. Yes, I do. Beyoncé is my favorite singer.
e. No, I don't. I don't have a computer.
f. Yes, I do. I like animals a lot.
g. No, I don't. I can't dance at all.
h. No, I don't. I'm not very artistic.

1 Check (✓) the word or phrase that is different.

1. ☑ use the Internet
   ☐ in-line skate
   ☐ dance
   ☐ play soccer

2. ☐ listen
   ☐ videos
   ☐ watch
   ☐ talk

3. ☐ collect stamps
   ☐ get up
   ☐ go to school
   ☐ go home

4. ☐ movie theater
   ☐ mall
   ☐ funny
   ☐ park

5. ☐ talk on the phone
   ☐ dangerous
   ☐ play video games
   ☐ watch DVDs

6. ☐ interesting
   ☐ Internet
   ☐ messy
   ☐ boring

7. ☐ Brazil
   ☐ Puerto Rico
   ☐ computer
   ☐ Canada

8. ☐ home
   ☐ school
   ☐ morning
   ☐ cafeteria

2 Complete the text with the verb phrases in the box.

| ☐ do my homework | ☐ eat dinner | ☑ get up | ☐ go to school | ☐ take dance lessons |
| ☐ eat breakfast | ☐ eat lunch | ☐ go to bed | ☐ listen to music | ☐ watch TV |

My name is Rosa. Every day, I _get up_ at
5:30 a.m. At 6:30, I _____ with my family.
Then I _____ . I walk with my sister and
brother. I _____ with my friend, Katie, in
the cafeteria. At 4:30, I _____ . I'm pretty
good at dancing. At 6:30, I _____ in the
dining room at home. Then I _____ . I
don't like homework very much. I like music a
lot. I _____ every night. Ilegales is my
favorite band. I don't _____ . TV is boring.
Then I _____ at 10:30.

3 Write sentences with your own information.

1. (watch TV) _I watch TV._ OR _I don't watch TV._
2. (play tennis) _____
3. (hang out at the park) _____
4. (in-line skate) _____
5. (write e-mail messages) _____
6. (get up at 6:30 a.m.) _____
7. (talk on the phone) _____
8. (speak three languages) _____

People I admire

1 Complete the chart with the correct forms of the verbs.

1. I work	she _works_	7. I live	she _____
2. I go	he _____	8. I take	he _____
3. I watch	she _____	9. I teach	she _____
4. I collect	he _____	10. I have	he _____
5. I guess	she _____	11. I make	she _____
6. I do	he _____	12. I practice	he _____

2 Complete the texts with the correct forms of the verbs in the box.

☐ do	☐ go	☐ listen	☐ talk	☐ work
☐ get up	☐ have	☑ live	☐ teach	☐ write

This is my cousin, Mary Ann. She's 13.
She _lives_ in Texas. She _____ at
6:30 every day. Then she _____ to school.
Mary Ann _____ hard in school.
Mrs. Haywood is Mary Ann's favorite
teacher. Mrs. Haywood _____ music.

After school, Mary Ann _____ her
homework and _____ to music in her
room. She _____ a computer in her
room. At night, she _____ on the phone
or _____ e-mail messages to her friends.

3 Write sentences about your friends or family members.

1. (talk) _My brother talks on the phone every day._
2. (work) _____
3. (read) _____
4. (collect) _____
5. (have) _____
6. (go to bed) _____
7. (play) _____
8. (get up) _____

The weekend

1 **Write sentences about the things Isabel doesn't do in her free time.**

1. Isabel plays video games.

   (the piano) *She doesn't play the piano.*

2. Isabel eats out with her family.

   (her friends) _____

3. She goes to the movies with her sister.

   (her brother) _____

4. Isabel likes candy.

   (popcorn) _____

5. On Saturday, Isabel sleeps late.

   (get up early) _____

6. She in-line skates in the park.

   (at school) _____

2 **Write negative sentences with *doesn't*.**

1. Adina watches TV in the dining room.   *Adina doesn't watch TV in the dining room.*

2. He goes to the movies every Saturday. _____

3. Gregorio stays home on Sunday. _____

4. She sleeps late on Monday. _____

5. Julio talks on the phone at school. _____

6. Gina goes out on Friday night. _____

7. He hangs out at the mall. _____

8. She collects stamps. _____

1 **Read the article quickly. Who's Abigail Breslin?**

_____

Slade Pearce and Abigail Breslin

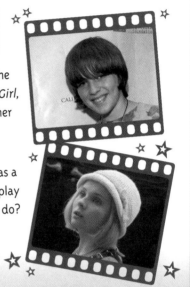

Slade Pearce, 13, is an actor on the TV show *October Road*. Slade gets up at 5:00 a.m. He eats breakfast and then at 6:00 a.m. he goes to the set of his TV show. On the set, he reviews his lines, and then he practices his part with the other actors on the show.

Slade doesn't go to a typical school. He goes to school on the set. Teen actors like Slade study with a special teacher for three to five hours every day on

the set. Abigail Breslin, the star of the movie *Kit Kittredge: An American Girl*, also goes to school on the set, but her parents teach her at home, too.

At home these actors are like other teens. Abigail loves animals. She has a big dog and two cats. She likes to play with them. What does Slade like to do? Slade likes computers and likes to send e-mail messages to his friends.

2 **Complete the sentences with the words in the box.**

☐ actor ☐ message ☐ practice ☐ review ☑ set

1. People make TV programs and movies on a ___set___ .

2. I have a _____ about the party in my e-mail inbox.

3. Do you _____ the guitar every day?

4. Who's your favorite _____ in the movies?

5. Let's _____ the new vocabulary words.

3 **Read the article in Part 1 slowly. Are these sentences true or false? Write *T* (true) or *F* (false). Then correct the false sentences.**

1. Slade Pearce goes to the set at 5:00 a.m. ___F___
   He doesn't go to the set at 5:00 a.m. He goes to the set at 6:00 a.m.

2. A special teacher teaches teen actors on a set. _____
   _____

3. Teen actors study on the set for ten hours every day. _____
   _____

4. Abigail Breslin doesn't like animals. _____
   _____

5. Slade Pearce writes e-mail messages to his friends. _____
   _____

Unit 2 Check Yourself

A Write sentences.

1. (Jess / in-line skate / after school) _Jess in-line skates after school._
2. (they / watch TV / 8:00) _____
3. (Kevin / not take dance lessons) _____
4. (Bridget / go out / Friday night) _____
5. (my father / not teach music) _____

B Write questions. Then answer the questions with your own information.

1. **Q:** (collect stamps) _Do you collect stamps?_

   A: _Yes, I do._ OR _No, I don't._

2. **Q:** (listen to music) _____

   A: _____

3. **Q:** (play video games) _____

   A: _____

4. **Q:** (watch DVDs) _____

   A: _____

C Max talks about his day. What does he say? Look at the time line. Check (✓) T (true) or F (false). Then correct the false sentences.

6:00	7:00	8:00	3:30	4:00	6:30	7:30	10:00
▲	▲	▲	▲	▲	▲	▲	▲
get up	eat breakfast at home	go to school with my sister	go home	play tennis	eat dinner	do homework	go to bed

	T	F	
1. I go to school with my mother.	☐	✓	_I don't go to school with my mother._ _I go to school with my sister._
2. I do my homework at 10:00.	☐	☐	
3. I eat breakfast at home.	☐	☐	
4. I play the piano at 4:00.	☐	☐	
5. I get up at 6:00.	☐	☐	

Lesson 9

Sports fun

1 Ann and Kay talk about their new gym teacher. Write conversations.

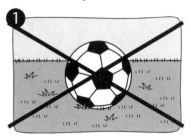
Ann *Does he play soccer?*
Kay *No, he doesn't.*

Ann _____
Kay _____

Ann _____
Kay _____

Ann _____
Kay _____

Ann _____
Kay _____

Ann _____
Kay _____

2 Write questions and answers.

1. **Q:** (Miss Alvarez / do karate) *Does Miss Alvarez do karate?*
   A: (yes) *Yes, she does.*

2. **Q:** (he / ski) _____
   A: (no) _____

3. **Q:** (Hiro / go biking) _____
   A: (yes / he) _____

4. **Q:** (Sarah / water-ski) _____
   A: (no / she) _____

5. **Q:** (she / surf) _____
   A: (yes) _____

6. **Q:** (Raul / skateboard) _____
   A: (no / he) _____

7. **Q:** (Angela / swim) _____
   A: (yes / she) _____

8. **Q:** (Mr. Miller / play baseball) _____
   A: (yes) _____

1 Write questions and answers.

1. (skiers / gloves)

   Q: *Do skiers wear gloves?*

   A: *Yes, they do. Skiers wear gloves.*

2. (cyclists / ski boots)

   Q: _____

   A: _____

3. (skateboarders / knee pads)

   Q: _____

   A: _____

4. (basketball players / hats)

   Q: _____

   A: _____

5. (swimmers / goggles)

   Q: _____

   A: _____

6. (baseball players / uniforms)

   Q: _____

   A: _____

7. (soccer players / hats)

   Q: _____

   A: _____

8. (cyclists / helmets)

   Q: _____

   A: _____

2 Complete the conversation. Write questions with *Do they* and the verb phrases in the box.

☐ play on a field   ☐ wear goggles   ☑ wear uniforms
☐ use knee pads   ☐ wear helmets

Jim Let's play a game. Guess my favorite sports team!

Andy OK. Let's see. Tell me about the players.
Do they wear uniforms?

Jim Yes, they do. They wear team uniforms.

Andy _____

Jim No, they don't wear helmets.

Andy _____

Jim No, they don't wear goggles.

Andy Wow! This is hard.

_____

Jim No, they don't. They don't use knee pads.

Andy _____

Jim No, they don't. They play on a court.

Andy Aha! Are they basketball players?

Jim Yes, they are! Our school basketball team is my
favorite. I'm on the team!

Mini-review

1 Check (✓) the word or phrase that is different.

1. ☐ basketball
   ☐ soccer
   ☑ piano
   ☐ tennis

2. ☐ knee pads
   ☐ stamps
   ☐ goggles
   ☐ gloves

3. ☐ uniform
   ☐ eyes
   ☐ feet
   ☐ head

4. ☐ athletic
   ☐ smart
   ☐ use
   ☐ artistic

5. ☐ skateboarder
   ☐ baseball player
   ☐ swimmer
   ☐ hat

6. ☐ swim
   ☐ write
   ☐ surf
   ☐ water-ski

7. ☐ park
   ☐ field
   ☐ helmet
   ☐ court

8. ☐ active
   ☐ go out
   ☐ sleep late
   ☐ stay home

2 Number the sentences in the correct order.

_____ No, he doesn't water-ski. But he skis in the winter.

_____ Does he surf?

_1_ Hey, there's Eduardo. He swims really well.

_____ Wow! He does a lot!

_____ Yeah, he's a good swimmer. He really likes the water.

_____ Yes, he's very athletic. He does a lot of sports.

_____ Every day? Wow! Does he water-ski, too?

_____ Yes, he does. He surfs every day in the summer.

**3 Circle the correct words to complete the questions.
Then write answers.**

1. A (**Do** / Does) your friends play soccer?
   B _Yes, they do._

2. A (Do / Does) you have goggles?
   B (no) _____

3. A (Do / Does) your teacher use the Internet?
   B (yes) _____

4. A (Do / Does) your best friend wear a hat?
   B (no) _____

4 Complete the questions with _Do_ or _Does_. Then answer the questions with your own information.

1. ___Do___ you like English?   _Yes, I do._

2. _____ your mother water-ski?   _____

3. _____ your best friend surf?   _____

4. _____ your classmates like homework? _____

Off to camp

1 Circle the correct words to complete the sentences.

1. I need a (pillow / boot) for my bed.

2. We need a (towel / raincoat) and some soap in the bathroom.

3. I can't see. Please, give me your (blanket / flashlight).

4. It's hot. I don't need a (blanket / pillow).

5. The camp rules say, "Bring a (dress / raincoat)."

2 Complete the conversation with the words in the box and the imperative.

☐ bring an MP3 player   ☐ use bug repellent   ☐ use sunscreen   ☑ wear sneakers

☐ bring a sleeping bag   ☐ bring your cell phone   ☑ wear hiking boots

Counselor OK, everyone. These are the rules for the hike today. First,
wear hiking boots . _Don't wear sneakers._ That's rule one.

Camper How about MP3 players?

Counselor _____ You can't listen to the MP3 player on the hike. Oh, and
_____ . You can call your friends after the hike.

Camper Are there any bugs?

Counselor Yes there are. Please, _____ . You need it. _____ , too.
It's very sunny today.

Camper Do we need sleeping bags?

Counselor No, _____ . This is a short hike. OK, let's go! Hiking is fun!

3 What are the rules in your class? Write imperatives.

1. (cell phones) _Don't bring cell phones._

2. (MP3 players) _____

3. (video games) _____

4. (the Internet) _____

5. (homework) _____

6. (comic books) _____

7. (guitar) _____

8. (magazines) _____

At camp

1 **Look at Marco's camp schedule. Answer the questions.**

9:30 – go canoeing	3:15 – do arts and crafts
10:45 – take swimming lessons	6:00 – make a campfire
12:30 – go horseback riding	6:30 – cook hot dogs
1:45 – go hiking	8:00 – tell stories

1. What time does Marco go canoeing? _He goes canoeing at 9:30._ OR _At 9:30._
2. When do the campers make a campfire? _____
3. What time does Marco go horseback riding? _____
4. What time do the campers go hiking? _____
5. When do they tell stories? _____
6. When does Marco take swimming lessons? _____
7. What time does Marco cook hot dogs? _____
8. When do they do arts and crafts? _____

2 **Write the time of day.**

1. 9 p.m. _in the evening_   3. 11 a.m. _____   5. 3 p.m. _____
2. 4 a.m. _____   4. 6 a.m. _____   6. 12 a.m. _____

3 **Write questions and answers.**

1. **Q:** (your parents / get up) _When do your parents get up?_
   A: (in the morning) _My parents get up in the morning._ OR _In the morning._

2. **Q:** (your friends / eat lunch) _____
   A: (in the afternoon) _____

3. **Q:** (your classmates / go home) _____
   A: (2:30) _____

4. **Q:** (your teacher / use his computer) _____
   A: (in the morning) _____

5. **Q:** (your sister / go to bed) _____
   A: (10:30) _____

6. **Q:** (your best friend / do homework) _____
   A: (in the evening) _____

Get Connected

1 **Read the Web site quickly. What's Tara's nickname?**

_____

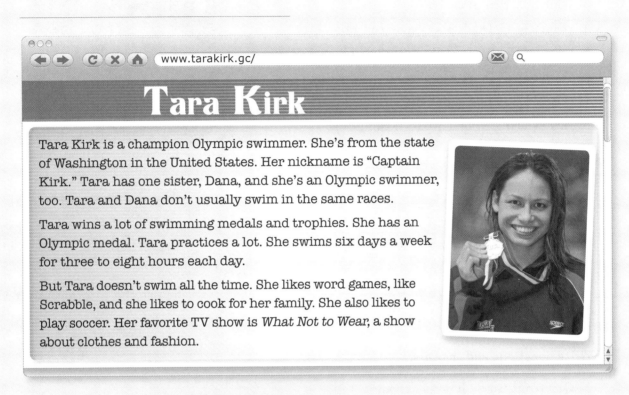

www.tarakirk.gc/

Tara Kirk

Tara Kirk is a champion Olympic swimmer. She's from the state of Washington in the United States. Her nickname is "Captain Kirk." Tara has one sister, Dana, and she's an Olympic swimmer, too. Tara and Dana don't usually swim in the same races.

Tara wins a lot of swimming medals and trophies. She has an Olympic medal. Tara practices a lot. She swims six days a week for three to eight hours each day.

But Tara doesn't swim all the time. She likes word games, like Scrabble, and she likes to cook for her family. She also likes to play soccer. Her favorite TV show is _What Not to Wear_, a show about clothes and fashion.

2 **Complete the sentences with the words in the box.**

☐ champion ☑ medals ☐ races ☐ trophies ☐ win

1. Michael Phelps is a famous Olympic swimmer. He has a lot of ___medals___ .

2. They have 10 points and we have 20. We _____ the game!

3. Let's watch the swimming _____ on TV today.

4. Brenda's very good at sports. She's a _____ .

5. My school's soccer team is really good. They have many _____ .

3 **Read the Web site in Part 1 slowly. Answer the questions.**

1. Is Tara Kirk from California? _No, she isn't. She's from Washington._

2. Do Tara and her sister swim in the same races? _____

3. Does Tara practice every day? _____

4. Does Tara like word games? _____

5. Is _What Not to Wear_ a TV show about fashion? _____

A Circle the correct words to complete the sentences.

1. ((Don't listen to)/ Don't get up) your radio at night.
2. (Listen to / Wear) sunscreen.
3. (Get up / Bring) early.
4. (Don't use / Don't play) your cell phone.
5. (Wear / Play) something comfortable.
6. (Don't eat / Don't wear) candy every day.
7. (Use / Play) bug repellent.
8. (Don't bring / Don't wear) a computer.

B Complete the sentences with *do, does, don't,* or *doesn't.*

1. **Q:** _____Do_____ cyclists wear helmets?
   A: Yes, they ___do___ .

2. **Q:** _____ she play baseball?
   A: No, she _____ .

3. **Q:** _____ he do karate?
   A: Yes, he _____ .

4. **Q:** _____ they wear knee pads?
   A: No, they _____ .

5. **Q:** _____ you skateboard?
   A: Yes, I _____ .

6. **Q:** _____ he use the Internet at school?
   A: No, he _____ .

C Write questions and answers.

1. **Q:** (What time / he / go canoeing?) _What time does he go canoeing?_
   A: (8:15) _He goes canoeing at 8:15_ OR _At 8:15._

2. **Q:** (When / she / do arts and crafts?) _____
   A: (in the afternoon) _____

3. **Q:** (What time / they / go hiking?) _____
   A: (10:00) _____

4. **Q:** (When / they / make a campfire?) _____
   A: (in the evening) _____

5. **Q:** (What time / she / go horseback riding?) _____
   A: (3:15) _____

6. **Q:** (When / he / tell stories?) _____
   A: (at night) _____

7. **Q:** (What time / you / take swimming lessons?) _____
   A: (9:30) _____

1 Complete the puzzle.

1. Sean Paul sings _reggae_ music.
2. Bon Jovi is a _____ musician.
3. Pink is a _____ singer.
4. The Dixie Chicks sing _____ music.
5. Kanye West sings _____ .
6. Joshua Bell is a _____ musician.

Complete the question with the mystery word.

What are your favorite music _____ ?

¹R	E	G	G	A	E		
			²R				
		³P					
	⁴C						
	⁵H						
⁶C							

2 Match the questions to the answers.

1. Do you listen to jazz? _d_
2. Do you like classical music? ____
3. Do you like the Jonas Brothers? ____
4. What's your favorite kind of music? ____
5. Who's your favorite country singer? ____
6. Who's your favorite musician? ____

a. Martina McBride is my favorite country singer. I like her a lot.
b. My favorite musician is Joshua Bell. I really like him.
c. Reggae is my favorite kind of music. I really like it!
d. Yes, I do. Jazz is cool. I like it.
e. No, I don't. Classical music is boring.
f. Yes, they're OK. I like them.

3 Choose the correct words to complete the sentences.

1. Jennifer Lopez is a good singer. I like _her_ (them / her).
2. The Plain White T's are cool. I like _____ (them / him) a lot.
3. I don't like rock music at all. I don't listen to _____ (them / it).
4. Hip-hop singers are OK. I like _____ (her / them).
5. Pop music is great! I like _____ (her / it) a lot.
6. Sean Paul is my favorite singer. I like _____ (him / it) a lot.

4 Answer the questions with your own information.

1. Do you like English? _Yes, I do. I like it a lot!_
2. Do you like the Jonas Brothers? _____
3. Do you like video games? _____
4. Do you like movies? _____
5. Do you like music videos? _____
6. Do you like Sean Paul? _____
7. Do you like baseball? _____
8. Do you like pop music? _____

Let's look online.

1 Look at the picture. Then write questions.

1. **Q:** *How much are the puzzles?*
   A: They're $3.99 each.

2. **Q:** _____
   A: It's $89.75.

3. **Q:** _____
   A: They're $29.95 each.

4. **Q:** _____
   A: They're $18.00 each.

5. **Q:** _____
   A: It's $79.50.

6. **Q:** _____
   A: They're $12.98 each.

7. **Q:** _____
   A: It's $99.99.

8. **Q:** _____
   A: It's $69.25.

2 Write questions with *How much*. Then look at the picture and answer the questions.

1. (books)
   Q: *How much are the books?*
   A: *They're $18.69 each.*

2. (skateboard)
   Q: _____
   A: _____

3. (travel vests)
   Q: _____
   A: _____

4. (CDs)
   Q: _____
   A: _____

5. (telescope)
   Q: _____
   A: _____

6. (star map)
   Q: _____
   A: _____

1 Check (✓) the correct responses.

1. Do you like classical music?
   - ☑ Yes, I do. I like it a lot.
   - ☐ Yes, I do. I like them a lot.

2. Do you listen to the Dixie Chicks?
   - ☐ Yes, I do. I like her.
   - ☐ No, I don't. I don't like them.

3. Who's your favorite hip-hop singer?
   - ☐ Cee-Lo. I really like it.
   - ☐ Cee-Lo. I really like him.

4. Do you like Mylie Cyrus?
   - ☐ Well, I like her, but she's not my favorite singer.
   - ☐ They're boring. I don't like them at all.

5. What's your favorite kind of music?
   - ☐ Reggae is my favorite. I like him a lot.
   - ☐ Reggae is great. I really like it.

6. Do you like Justin Timberlake?
   - ☐ Yes, I do. He's my favorite.
   - ☐ Not really. They're boring.

7. Do you listen to Laura Pausini?
   - ☐ No, I don't. I don't like it.
   - ☐ No, I don't. I don't really like her.

8. What's your favorite rock group?
   - ☐ The Backstreet Boys are cool. I like them.
   - ☐ The Backstreet Boys are weird. I don't like them at all.

2 Complete the questions with *How much is* or *How much are*.

1. _How much is_ the CD?
2. _____ the goggles?
3. _____ the radio?
4. _____ the calendar?
5. _____ the travel vests?
6. _____ the adventure DVD?

3 Look at the information. Are these statements true or false? Write *T* (true) or *F* (false). Then correct the false statements.

1. The flashlights are $13.95 each. _F_
   They're $8.69 each.

2. The hiking boots are $69.00. _____
   _____

3. The soccer ball is $18.66. _____
   _____

4. The star maps are $49.22 each. _____
   _____

5. The experiment kit is $24.99. _____
   _____

6. The music books are $19.35 each. _____
   _____

- ☐ experiment kit $24.99
- ☑ flashlights $8.69 each
- ☐ hiking boots $69.00
- ☐ music books $13.95 each
- ☐ soccer ball $16.88
- ☐ star maps $22.49 each

Lesson 15 Our interests

1 Write sentences.

> ✓ = like to / likes to
> ✗ = don't like to / doesn't like to

1. go camping ✓ / go shopping ✗
   (I) _I like to go camping. I don't like_
   _____to go shopping._

2. ski ✓ / do crossword puzzles ✗
   (I) _____
   _____

3. write poetry ✓ / play tennis ✗
   (he) _____
   _____

4. play video games ✓ / practice the piano ✗
   (she) _____
   _____

5. go dancing ✓ / watch TV ✗
   (she) _____
   _____

6. go to the movies ✓ / do my homework ✗
   (I) _____
   _____

7. in-line skate ✓ / read magazines ✗
   (I) _____
   _____

8. spend time at the beach ✓ / hang out at the mall ✗
   (he) _____
   _____

2 Complete the sentences with *like to* or *don't like to* and the verb phrases in the box.

> do crossword puzzles   go camping   go shopping   listen to music

Eddie Hey, Al. What's that?

Al Hi, Eddie. It's a crossword puzzle.
I _like to do crossword puzzles_. They're interesting.

Eddie Me, too. I really like the outdoors, too.
I _____ in my free time. How about you?

Al Not me. I don't like the outdoors, so I
_____ . I like indoor activities.

Eddie Do you like to listen to music?

Al Yes, I do. I _____ . Rock and reggae are my favorites.

Eddie What don't you like to do?

Al That's easy. I _____ with my sister. She hangs out at the mall all day!

In and out of school

1 Match the words to make verb phrases.

1. answer ___d___   a. paper airplanes
2. come _____   b. my homework
3. do _____   c. to class on time
4. throw _____   d. the teacher's questions
5. sleep _____   e. in class
6. get _____   f. good grades

2 Choose the correct words to complete the sentences.

1. I like video games. I _sometimes_ (sometimes / hardly ever) play them.

2. I love country music. I _____ (never / always) listen to Shania Twain.

3. I'm not very athletic. I _____ (hardly ever / always) play sports.

4. I like to watch TV. I _____ (usually / never) watch TV every night.

5. Rock music is boring. I _____ (always / hardly ever) listen to it.

6. In my free time, I _____ (never / usually) spend time at the beach. I love the beach!

7. _____ (Sometimes / Hardly ever) I like to hang out with my best friend.

8. I go to school at 7:30 in the morning. I _____ (always / never) sleep late on weekdays.

3 Write sentences. Use your own information and *always, usually, sometimes, hardly ever,* or *never.*

1. (throw paper airplanes in English class)
   I never throw paper airplanes in English class.

2. (sing in class) _____

3. (get good grades) _____

4. (skateboard) _____

5. (listen to music) _____

6. (spend time at the beach) _____

7. (come to class on time) _____

8. (do karate) _____

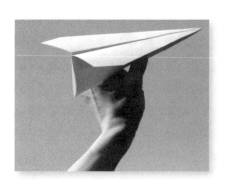

My Interests   27

1 **Read the article quickly. Where are the people in This Ambitious Orchestra from?**

_____

A New Kind of Music

You like rock music. But do you like classical music, too? People usually think that rock music and classical music are very different. This isn't true for the people in This Ambitious Orchestra of New York City.

This Ambitious Orchestra is a group of 20 classical musicians, but they play rock music. There are violins and other classical instruments in the orchestra, but they have electric guitars and drums, too. They have a new and exciting sound.

The musicians in This Ambitious Orchestra sometimes like to write their own music. They connect rock music and classical music in the music they write.

Teenagers and their parents both like to come to the concerts. And both teens and parents download songs by This Ambitious Orchestra on the Internet. The group also sells their album, _The Ambitious Orchestra._

2 **Check (✓) the correct words to complete the sentences.**

1. People usually think the violin is ☐ an electric   ☑ a classical   music instrument.

2. Do you have the Jonas Brothers' new ☐ album?   ☐ musician?

3. Let's ☐ download   ☐ sell   that song from the Internet.

4. Do they ☐ download   ☐ sell   those CDs in that store?

5. He plays the piano and the guitar. He's a great ☐ album.   ☐ musician.

3 **Read the article in Part 1 slowly. Are these sentences true or false? Write _T_ (true) or _F_ (false). Then correct the false sentences.**

1. There are 30 musicians in This Ambitious Orchestra. _F_
   There are 20 musicians in This Ambitious Orchestra.

2. This Ambitious Orchestra plays rock music with classical instruments. _____

   _____

3. The people in This Ambitious Orchestra always write their own music. _____

   _____

4. Parents don't like to come to the orchestra's concerts. _____

   _____

5. This Ambitious Orchestra sells songs on the Internet. _____

A Rewrite the sentences with *her*, *him*, *it*, or *them*.

1. Mario likes Pink. _Mario likes her._
2. We like the Dixie Chicks a lot. _____
3. Peter doesn't like hip-hop. _____
4. I don't really like jazz. _____
5. Eric listens to Sean Paul all the time. _____
6. She doesn't like Joshua Redman at all. _____

B Complete the questions with *How much is* or *How much are*. Then answer the questions.

1. **Q:** _How much is_ _____ the star map?

   A: ($12.75) _It's $12.75._ _____

2. **Q:** _____ the adventure DVDs?

   A: ($22.99 each) _____

3. **Q:** _____ the wall calendar?

   A: ($14.75) _____

4. **Q:** _____ the puzzles?

   A: ($8.00 each) _____

5. **Q:** _____ the travel vest?

   A: ($67.50) _____

6. **Q:** _____ the telescopes?

   A: ($49.95 each) _____

C Complete the sentences with the correct words.

1. I _don't like to go_ (like to go / don't like to go) shopping. It's boring.
2. I'm a very active person. I _____ (like to spend / don't like to spend) time outdoors.
3. I don't like sports. I _____ (like to play / don't like to play) soccer.
4. I _____ (never / usually) go out on Saturday. I hardly ever stay home.
5. I really like English class. I _____ (always / never) sleep in class.
6. I _____ (sometimes / hardly ever) eat hamburgers. I don't like them very much.
7. I like quiet indoor activities. I _____ (like to write / don't like to write) poetry.

In San Francisco

1 Label the pictures with the verb phrases in the box.

☐ go sightseeing ☐ see a show ☐ take pictures
☑ ride a trolley ☐ take a boat ride ☐ walk in the park

1. _ride a trolley_   2. _____   3. _____

4. _____   5. _____   6. _____

2 Write these sentences in the present continuous.

1. You walk. _You're walking._   5. She goes. _____
2. They buy. _____   6. I write. _____
3. We take. _____   7. They do. _____
4. I ride. _____   8. We practice. _____

3 Write these sentences in the present continuous.

1. (they / take a boat ride) _They're taking a boat ride._
2. (he / buy souvenirs) _____
3. (we / go sightseeing) _____
4. (she / walk in the park) _____
5. (they / see a show) _____
6. (I / take pictures) _____
7. (you / visit a museum) _____
8. (we / ride a trolley) _____

4 What are you doing right now? Write four sentences in the present continuous.
Use your own information.

1. _____   3. _____
2. _____   4. _____

1 Complete the sentences to make negative statements. Use the correct forms of the verb phrases in the box.

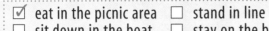

☑ eat in the picnic area ☐ stand in line ☐ throw trash in the trash can
☐ sit down in the boat ☐ stay on the bike path ☐ wait for the green light

1. They *aren't eating in the picnic area* . 2. She _____ .

3. He _____ . 4. I'm _____ .

5. We _____ . 6. He _____ .

2 Write sentences.   ✓ = is doing something   ✗ = isn't doing something

1. he / pay attention ✗ / read a comic book ✓
   He isn't paying attention. He's reading a comic book.

2. we / follow the rules ✗ / throw paper airplanes ✓
   _____

3. I / read a magazine ✗ / use the Internet ✓
   _____

4. she / write poetry ✗ / listen to music ✓
   _____

5. they / stand in line ✗ / walk in the park ✓
   _____

6. he / practice the piano ✗ / play video games ✓
   _____

1 **Complete the crossword puzzle with the words in the box.**

☐ bike ☐ picnic ☐ show ☐ standing ☐ visiting
☐ boat ☐ pictures ☑ souvenirs ☐ trash ☐ waiting

Across
3. We're buying _____souvenirs_____ .
5. They're seeing a _____ .
7. He isn't staying on the _____ path.
9. I'm _____ in line.
10. She's taking _____ .

Down
1. She isn't sitting down in the _____ .
2. I'm throwing _____ in the trash can.
4. They're _____ a museum.
6. We aren't _____ for the green light.
8. He's eating in the _____ area.

```
        [1]              [2]
[3]S  O  U  [4]V  E  N  I  R  S
        |        |              [5]      [6]
        |        |              |         |
                 |        [7]
               [8]
[9]
        |        |
                 |
       [10]
```

2 **Look at the pictures. Then write sentences in the present continuous.**

1. Pedro and José / in-line skate

   Pedro and José aren't in-line skating. They're skateboarding.

2. Mia / stand in line

   _____

3. Cesar / walk in the park

   _____

4. Denise and Julia / eat in the picnic area

   _____

5. Raul / talk on a cell phone

   _____

6. Sherri / throw paper airplanes

   _____

At the beach

1 Answer the questions.

1. Is he playing in the sand?

No, he isn't. He's swimming in the ocean.

2. Are they collecting seashells?

_____

3. Are they flying a kite?

_____

4. Is she floating on a raft?

_____

5. Is he playing in the sand?

_____

6. Are they surfing?

_____

2 Write questions and answers.

1. **Q:** (Scott / play in the sand) *Is Scott playing in the sand?*   **A:** (no) *No, he isn't.*

2. **Q:** (Linda / float on a raft) _____   **A:** (yes) _____

3. **Q:** (Josh and Brian / sail a boat) _____   **A:** (no) _____

4. **Q:** (Sally / collect seashells) _____   **A:** (yes) _____

5. **Q:** (Alberto / swim in the ocean) _____   **A:** (no) _____

6. **Q:** (Natalie and Sasha / have a picnic) _____   **A:** (yes) _____

At the store

1 **Complete the puzzle with words in the pictures.**

✔

☐

☐

☐

☐

☐

					¹R	I	N	G	
²									
				³					
		⁴							
	⁵								
		⁶							

Find the "secret" word to complete the sentence.

I'm buying a tennis _____.

2 **Read the answers. Look at the underlined words. Then write questions.**

1. **Q:** _What are you shopping for?_
   A: I'm <u>shopping for</u> a hat.

2. **Q:** _____
   A: She's <u>buying</u> a bracelet.

3. **Q:** _____
   A: They're <u>looking at</u> surfboards.

4. **Q:** _____
   A: He's <u>trying on</u> a coat.

5. **Q:** _____
   A: She's <u>paying for</u> a necklace.

6. **Q:** _____
   A: I'm <u>buying</u> a tennis racket.

7. **Q:** _____
   A: We're <u>looking at</u> trading cards.

1 **Read the article quickly. Is Stacy having an exciting vacations?**

_____

A Special Vacation

These teens are on vacation, but this isn't a traditional vacation. They aren't sightseeing, visiting museums, or visiting old castles — they're working at a national park. They're collecting the trash in big bags. They're working in the picnic areas and on the bike paths. They're making the park a nice place for visitors. Stacy is 15 and she's spending two weeks at the park. She says:

"Right now some of my friends are on vacation in New York. They're seeing plays and shows and shopping for souvenirs. But I think this is more fun. We work, but we do fun things, too. We have picnics every day, and there's a great beach near the park. We go there sometimes. Today some of my friends are sailing and surfing at the beach. I'm taking a lot of pictures of all our activities. Pictures are good souvenirs. This is an exciting vacation. We're having fun, and we're helping the park, too."

2 **Complete the sentences with the words in the box.**

☐ castle   ☑ play   ☐ sailing   ☐ shopping   ☐ traditional

1. They're watching a _____play_____ at the theater.

2. The boys are _____ a boat in the ocean.

3. She's _____ for a new jacket.

4. They live in a big _____ . It's very old.

5. They're going camping in Africa. It's not a _____ vacation.

3 **Read the article in Part 1 slowly. Answer the questions.**

1. Are the teens sightseeing in the park? _No, they aren't. They're working in the park._

2. Are they working on the bike paths and in the picnic areas? _____

3. Is Stacy spending three weeks at the park? _____

4. Are Stacy's friends working at the beach today? _____

5. Is Stacy taking a lot pictures? _____

A Write affirmative present continuous sentences.

1. (I / take pictures) _I'm taking pictures._

2. (they / visit a museum) _____

3. (she / ride a trolley) _____

4. (he / throw trash in the trash can) _____

5. (we / wait for the green light) _____

6. (you / buy souvenirs) _____

B Write negative present continuous sentences.

1. I'm staying on the bike path.

    (we) _We aren't staying on the bike path._

2. He's standing in line.

    (they) _____

3. They're playing in the sand.

    (she) _____

4. We're going sightseeing.

    (he) _____

5. She's eating in the picnic area.

    (I) _____

6. I'm visiting a museum.

    (you) _____

C Write questions with *Is* or *Are*. Then answer the questions.

1. **Q:** (she / look at jackets) _Is she looking at jackets?_

    A: (no / shoes) _No, she isn't. She's looking at shoes._

2. **Q:** (he / buy comic books) _____

    A: (no / a scarf) _____

3. **Q:** (they / collect seashells) _____

    A: (yes) _____

4. **Q:** (they / throw a Frisbee) _____

    A: (no / fly a kite) _____

5. **Q:** (you / go sightseeing) _____

    A: (yes) _____

1 Look at the ads. Then write questions.

1. **Q:** *Where's she going?*

   A: She's going to a concert.

2. **Q:** _____

   A: They're going to an animal exhibit.

3. **Q:** _____

   A: He's going to the movies.

4. **Q:** _____

   A: I'm going to the circus.

5. **Q:** _____

   A: We're going to a soccer game.

6. **Q:** _____

   A: She's going to a science exhibit.

2 Write questions and answers with *be + going to*.

1. (Amy / the museum)

   Q: *Where's Amy going?*

   A: *She's going to the museum.*

2. (Mr. Parker / a concert)

   Q: _____

   A: _____

3. (Ava and Jenna / the mall)

   Q: _____

   A: _____

4. (you and Roberto / the soccer game)

   Q: _____

   A: _____

Birthday parties

1 Write the sentences in the present continuous.

1. We usually eat at home. (restaurant) _We're eating at a restaurant now._
2. He usually does homework. (write poetry) _____
3. They usually relax at home. (go to the movies) _____
4. I usually sing songs. (listen to music) _____
5. His sisters usually play cards. (hang out with friends) _____
6. We usually watch TV. (play party games) _____
7. They usually play baseball. (do karate) _____
8. She usually eats pizza. (eat cake) _____

2 It's Saturday at 11 a.m. Look at the chart. Then write sentences.

Name	Usually	Now
1. Antonio	sleep late	play cards
2. Tomas	watch TV	swim
3. Jack	do his homework	read a book
4. Marla	talk on the phone	listen to music
5. Kelly	relax at home	hang out at the mall
6. Jane	read magazines	use the Internet

1. _Antonio usually sleeps late. He's playing cards now._
2. _____
3. _____
4. _____
5. _____
6. _____

3 What do you do on your birthday? Write sentences with your own information.

1. _____
2. _____
3. _____
4. _____
5. _____
6. _____

Mini-review

1 **Complete the sentences with the correct forms of the verbs.**

1. Look! The athlete _is talking_ (talk) to her fans now.
2. Ashley usually _____ (stay) home on Saturday.
3. My sisters sometimes _____ (watch) TV after school.
4. Tom _____ (celebrate) his birthday now.
5. Gina _____ (eat) dinner at a restaurant now.
6. We usually _____ (have) a barbecue on Sunday.

2 **Look at the pictures. Then write questions and answers.**

1. **Q**: _Where's Dena going?_
   A: _She's going to the shoe store._
2. **Q**: _____
   A: _____

3. **Q**: _____
   A: _____
4. **Q**: _____
   A: _____

3 **What do these people do on the weekend? Look at the information in the chart. Are these statements true or false? Write _T_ (true) or _F_ (false). Then correct the false statements.**

Name	Usually	Now	Name	Usually	Now
1. Erica	watch TV	read a book	4. Edwin	eat dinner at home	eat at a restaurant
2. Alanna	play cards	sing songs	5. Kevin	practice the piano	float on a raft
3. Scott	skateboard	play video games	6. Alysha	go to the library	go to the circus

1. Erica usually reads books.   _F_   _Erica usually watches TV. She's reading_
   a book now.

2. Alanna is singing songs now. ____ _____

3. Scott is skateboarding now. ____ _____

4. Edwin usually eats at a restaurant. ____ _____

5. Kevin is floating on a raft now. ____ _____

6. Alysha usually goes to the circus. ____ _____

Let's see a movie.

1 Write the sentences in the correct order to make a conversation.

> ☐ Is it a documentary?   ☐ No, thanks. I want to see a comedy.
> ☑ I want to go to the movies.   ☐ What do you want to see?
> ☐ I want to see *Amazing Elephants*.   ☐ Yes, it is. Do you want to come?

A *I want to go to the movies.*

B _____

A _____

B _____

A _____

B _____

2 Look at the pictures. Then write sentences with *want to* and the words in the box.

> ☐ an action movie   ☐ a comedy   ☐ a drama
> ☐ an animated movie   ☑ a documentary   ☐ a horror movie

1. *We want to see a documentary.*

2. **A** _____

    B Yes, I do.

3. _____

4. **A** _____

    B No, I don't.

5. _____

6. _____

In line at the movies

1 **Check (✓) the correct words to complete the sentences.**

1. Veronica isn't heavy. She's ☑ slim. ☐ wavy.

2. Her hair is short. It isn't ☐ tall. ☐ long.

3. Her hair isn't straight. It's ☐ curly. ☐ brown.

4. She's average height. She isn't ☐ tall. ☐ long.

5. Her eyes are blue. They aren't ☐ blond. ☐ brown.

2 **Circle the correct words to complete the sentences. Then match the questions to the answers.**

1. What ((does)/ is) Tina look like? _b_   a. It's short and straight.

2. What's his (look / hair) like? ____   b. She's short and slim.

3. What (color / curly) is her hair? ____   c. He's tall and heavy.

4. What color (is / are) his eyes? ____   d. It's blond.

5. What does Ramon (is / look) like? ____   e. They're blue.

3 **Write questions.**

1. **Q:** (Aleta) _What does Aleta look like?_

   A: Aleta is average height and slim.

2. **Q:** (Don) _____

   A: They're blue.

3. **Q:** (Viviana) _____

   A: It's brown.

4. **Q:** (Allen) _____

   A: It's short and curly.

5. **Q:** (Paco) _____

   A: Paco is tall and heavy.

6. **Q:** (Sara) _____

   A: It's blond and wavy.

4 **Answer the questions with your own information.**

1. What do you look like? _____

2. What color are your eyes? _____

3. What's your hair like? _____

4. What color is your hair? _____

5. What does your best friend look like? _____

6. What's your teacher's hair like? _____

1 **Read the e-mail quickly. How many bats are in one place in Texas?**

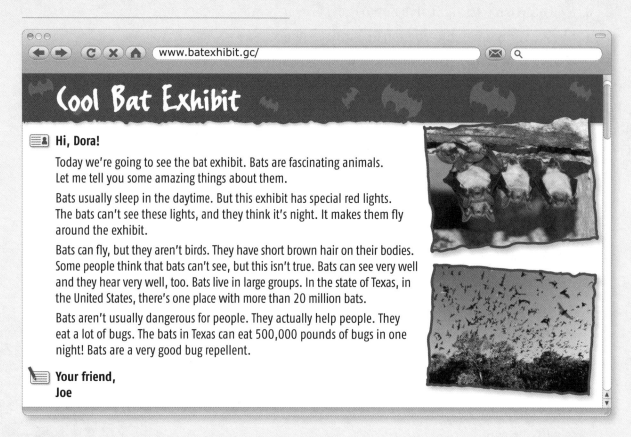

www.batexhibit.gc/

Cool Bat Exhibit

Hi, Dora!

Today we're going to see the bat exhibit. Bats are fascinating animals. Let me tell you some amazing things about them.

Bats usually sleep in the daytime. But this exhibit has special red lights. The bats can't see these lights, and they think it's night. It makes them fly around the exhibit.

Bats can fly, but they aren't birds. They have short brown hair on their bodies. Some people think that bats can't see, but this isn't true. Bats can see very well and they hear very well, too. Bats live in large groups. In the state of Texas, in the United States, there's one place with more than 20 million bats.

Bats aren't usually dangerous for people. They actually help people. They eat a lot of bugs. The bats in Texas can eat 500,000 pounds of bugs in one night! Bats are a very good bug repellent.

Your friend,
Joe

2 **Complete the sentences with the words in the box.**

| ☐ exhibit | ☑ fascinating | ☐ hair | ☐ million | ☐ pounds |

1. Dogs are _fascinating_ animals. They're very interesting.

2. Let's go to the _____ on snakes.

3. There are about 8 _____ people in New York City.

4. We need two _____ of apples for the pies.

5. Bert has black _____ and brown eyes.

3 **Read the e-mail in Part 1 slowly. Answer the questions.**

1. Where are the campers going today? _They're going to the nature center._

2. What do bats do in the daytime? _____

3. Can the bats see the red lights? _____

4. What's a bat's hair like? _____

5. What do bats eat? _____

A Write questions and answers.

1. **Q:** *Where are you going?*

   A: I'm going to the science exhibit.

2. **Q:** _____

   A: He's short and heavy.

3. **Q:** _____

   A: It's black.

4. **Q:** I want to go shopping. Do you want to come?

   A: (yes) _____

5. **Q:** Where's she going?

   A: (movie festival) _____

6. **Q:** What kind of movie do you want to see?

   A: (action movie) _____

B What do these people usually do on Saturday afternoon? What are they doing now? Write sentences.

1. eat hamburgers / eat pizza

   (we) *We usually eat hamburgers. We're eating pizza now.*

   _____

2. watch TV / go to a concert

   (we) _____

   _____

3. read a book / have a barbecue

   (Mr. Goldman) _____

   _____

4. go to a basketball game / in-line skate

   (Karla) _____

   _____

5. play baseball / relax at home

   (he) _____

   _____

6. hang out at the mall / visit a museum

   (they) _____

UNIT 7 What We Eat

1 Label the photos. Then write *C* if the food is countable and *U* if the food is uncountable.

1. _____apples_____ _C_

2. _____

3. _____

4.
_____

5.
_____

6.
_____

7. _____

8.
_____

2 Choose the correct words to complete the sentences.

1. He's buying _____water_____ (banana / water).
2. She wants _____ (meat / cookie) for dinner.
3. There are five _____ (broccoli / potatoes).
4. They don't eat _____ (hot dogs / egg).
5. There's _____ (butter / apples) on the table.
6. He's eating _____ (apple / rice).
7. How about a _____ (cheese / sandwich)?
8. I want five _____ (apples / meat).

3 Write sentences with the correct forms of the nouns and your own information.

1. (ice cream) _I like ice cream._
2. (banana) _____
3. (broccoli) _____
4. (butter) _____
5. (hot dog) _____
6. (cheese) _____

Picnic plans

1 **Complete the sentences with *how much*, *how many*, *a little*, *a lot*, or *a few*.**

1. *How many* plates do we have?
2. There's _____ bread.
3. We have _____ of pasta.
4. _____ milk is there?

5. There are _____ of knives and spoons.
6. _____ cheese do we have?
7. There are only _____ cups.
8. _____ bananas do we need?

2 **Look at the picture. Then write sentences about the quantities of the items with *We have*.**

1. (fruit) *We have a lot of fruit.*
2. (forks) _____
3. (pasta) _____

4. (milk) _____
5. (cups) _____
6. (spoons) _____

3 **Write questions and answers. Use *Is there* or *Are there*.**

1. (cups / five)
   Q: *How many cups are there?*
   A: *There are five cups.*

2. (knives / eight)
   Q: _____
   A: _____

3. (forks / six)
   Q: _____
   A: _____

4. (juice / a little)
   Q: _____
   A: _____

5. (bread / a lot)
   Q: _____
   A: _____

6. (pasta / a lot)
   Q: _____
   A: _____

1 Look at the chart. Complete the questions. Then answer the questions.

Name		A lot	A little	A few
Alice		✓		
Jean and Joe				✓
Tony			✓	
Ivy and Jan		✓		
Nancy				✓
Ruben			✓	

1. **Q:** _How much bread_ does Alice have?
   A: _She has a lot of bread._

2. **Q:** _____ do Jean and Joe want?
   A: _____

3. **Q:** _____ does Tony need?
   A: _____

4. **Q:** _____ do Ivy and Jan need?
   A: _____

5. **Q:** _____ does Nancy want?
   A: _____

6. **Q:** _____ does Ruben have?
   A: _____

2 Write questions with *How much* or *How many*.

1. **Q:** _How much juice do you drink every day?_
   A: I drink a little juice every day.

2. **Q:** _____
   A: I have three brothers.

3. **Q:** _____
   A: I eat a little fruit every morning.

4. **Q:** _____
   A: I read a few comic books every month.

5. **Q:** _____
   A: I eat two cookies after school.

6. **Q:** _____
   A: I drink a lot of water in the morning.

1 Number the sentences in the correct order.

_____ Sorry, I don't like mayonnaise at all.

_____ Sure. Jelly burgers are my favorite!

__1__ Let's make hamburgers.

_____ I don't like mustard. Hey! There's some pepper and some jelly.

_____ That's okay. We have some mustard, but there isn't any ketchup.

_____ What? Jelly on a hamburger?

_____ Me, too. Let's use some mayonnaise.

_____ Good idea! I'm really hungry.

2 Look at the picture. Then write sentences with *some* or *any*.

1. _There aren't any sandwiches._

2. _____

3. _____

4. _____

5. _____

6. _____

3 Are these items in your kitchen? Check (✓) Yes or No. Then write sentences.

	Yes	No	
1. salt	✓	☐	_There's some salt._
2. jelly	☐	☐	_____
3. ketchup	☐	☐	_____
4. mayonnaise	☐	☐	_____
5. pepper	☐	☐	_____
6. ham	☐	☐	_____

On the menu

1 **Complete the chart with the words in the box.**

☐ baked potato ☐ cheeseburger ☐ fish ☐ iced tea ☐ soda
☑ black bean soup ☐ chicken sandwich ☐ French fries ☐ milk shake ☐ steak sandwich
☐ carrot cake ☐ chocolate cake ☐ ice cream ☐ salad ☐ vegetable soup

Appetizers	Main dishes	Side orders	Desserts	Drinks
black bean soup				

2 **Write questions and answers.**

1. **Q:** (an appetizer) *Would you like an appetizer?*
   A: Yes, please. I'd like black bean soup.

2. **Q:** (drink) _____
   A: I'd like a milk shake.

3. **Q:** (ice cream) _____
   A: No, thanks. I don't like ice cream.

4. **Q:** Would you like a main dish?
   A: (fish) _____

5. **Q:** Would you like a side order?
   A: (no) _____

3 **Complete the questions with *Do you like* or *Would you like*.**

1. **A** *Do you like* chocolate cake?
   B Yes. I love it.

   A *Would you like* some chocolate cake now?
   B No, thanks. I'm not hungry.

2. **A** _____ some iced tea with your sandwich?
   B Yes, please. I'm thirsty.

3. **A** _____ soda?
   B No, I don't. It isn't a healthy drink.

4. **A** _____ pie?
   B Yes. I like apple pie.

5. **A** _____ some mustard on your cheeseburger?
   B Yes, and I'd like some ketchup, too.

1 Read the article quickly. Is it easy to eat a Dagwood?

_____

How to Make a Dagwood

A Dagwood is a kind of sandwich. It gets its name from Dagwood Bumstead. He's one of the main characters in the _Blondie_ comics. You can read _Blondie_ comics in newspapers all over the world. The comic is more than 75 years old.

Dagwood doesn't like to work. He likes to sleep, and he likes to eat. He loves to make sandwiches. In the comics, Dagwood often gets hungry and goes into the kitchen. He opens the refrigerator, takes out a lot of food, and makes a very big sandwich. There's no recipe for a Dagwood. There's always a lot of meat and cheese in the sandwich and usually some lettuce and other vegetables. Sometimes Dagwood puts bananas, apples, or other kinds of fruit in the sandwich, too. He always uses a lot of mustard, mayonnaise, and ketchup. But, there's one problem with a Dagwood sandwich. It isn't easy to eat it. It's really big!

2 Complete the sentences with the words in the box.

| ☐ fruit | ☑ ketchup | ☐ newspaper | ☐ recipe | ☐ refrigerator |

1. Please put a lot of ____ketchup____ on my hamburger.

2. The milk is in the _____ .

3. Do you have a good _____ for chocolate cake?

4. There's an interesting article about food in the _____ today.

5. An apple is a healthy _____ .

3 Read the article in Part 1 slowly. Check (✓) the correct words to complete the sentences.

1. You can find _Blondie_ comics _____ .
   - ☐ only in the United States
   - ☐ all over the world

2. Dagwood Bumstead likes to _____ .
   - ☐ work and sleep
   - ☐ sleep and eat

3. _____ for a Dagwood sandwich.
   - ☐ There's no recipe
   - ☐ There are two recipes

4. There's always a lot of _____ in a Dagwood.
   - ☐ fruit and vegetables
   - ☐ meat and cheese

5. It's difficult to eat a Dagwood. The sandwich _____ .
   - ☐ is very big
   - ☐ has no mayonnaise on it

A **Complete these questions with *How much* or *How many*. Then match the questions to the answers.**

1. _How many_ CDs do you have? __e__   a. I drink a lot of juice every day.

2. _____ soda do we have? ____   b. We need eight cups.

3. _____ hours do you sleep every night? ____   c. I speak three languages.

4. _____ cups do we need? ____   d. We have a little soda.

5. _____ languages do you speak? ____   e. I have a lot of CDs.

6. _____ juice do you drink every day? ____   f. I sleep eight hours every night.

B **Complete the sentences with the correct words.**

1. _There isn't_ (There isn't / There aren't) ____any____ (some / any) milk.

2. _____ (There's / There are) _____ (some / any) cups.

3. _____ (There's some / There are some) _____ (eggs / egg).

4. _____ (There's / There are) _____ (some / any) chicken.

5. _____ (There are some / There's some) _____ (potatoes / potato).

C **Write questions with *Would you like*. Then answer the questions with your own information.**

1. **Q:** (dessert) _Would you like some dessert?_

   A: _Yes, please. I'd like some ice cream._

2. **Q:** (a drink) _____

   A: _____

3. **Q:** (a hamburger) _____

   A: _____

4. **Q:** (soup) _____

   A: _____

5. **Q:** (an appetizer) _____

   A: _____

6. **Q:** (pizza) _____

   A: _____

1 Check (✓) the correct words to complete the sentences.

1. It isn't cold today. It's ☐ snowy. ☑ hot.

2. It isn't sunny today. It's ☐ warm. ☐ cloudy.

3. It's cloudy today, and it's ☐ sunny, ☐ rainy, too.

4. It's cold today, and it's ☐ windy, ☐ warm, too.

2 Look at the pictures. Write sentences.

1. _It's hot and sunny today._____   2. _____

3. _____   4. _____

5. _____   6. _____

3 Write questions and answers.

1. **Q:** (Chicago / January) _What's the weather like in Chicago in January?_

   A: It's usually cold and snowy.

2. **Q:** (Miami / August) _____

   A: It's usually hot and rainy.

3. **Q:** What's the weather like in Sydney in May?

   A: (warm / cloudy) _____

4. **Q:** (New York City / today) _____

   A: It's cool and windy today.

5. **Q:** What's the weather like in Tokyo in December?

   A: (cold / sunny) _____

Natural wonders

1 **Complete the sentences with the correct words.**

1. You can climb an incredible ___mountain___ (river / mountain) in this park.
2. This _____ (island / cave) is usually hot and rainy in June.
3. Can you relax in a _____ (mountain / hot spring) in this park?
4. You can see bats in this _____ (hotel / cave).
5. You can live in a houseboat on a _____ (hot spring / river).

2 **Write questions.**

1. **Q:** _What can you see in a rain forest?_

   A: You can see fascinating birds and animals in a rain forest.

2. **Q:** _____

   A: Yes, you can. You can see bats in a cave.

3. **Q:** _____

   A: Yes, you can. You can buy food and souvenirs at hotels.

4. **Q:** _____

   A: No, you can't. You can't collect seashells in the mountains.

5. **Q:** _____

   A: You can see birds on this island.

6. **Q:** _____

   A: You can go camping in this park.

3 **Answer the questions.**

1. **Q:** Can you see bears on this trail?

   A: (no / snakes and spiders) _No, you can't. You can see snakes and spiders._

2. **Q:** Can you buy food around here?

   A: (yes / the hotel) _____

3. **Q:** What can you do on this river?

   A: (go canoeing) _____

4. **Q:** Can you go camping in this park?

   A: (no / hiking) _____

5. **Q:** What can you do in the hot spring?

   A: (sit and relax) _____

6. **Q:** What can you see on this island?

   A: (an underground cave) _____

Mini-review

1 Look at the chart. Then write questions and answers.

	Buenos Aires, Argentina	**Tokyo, Japan**
January	hot / rainy	cold / cloudy
April	warm / cloudy	cool / sunny
August	cool / sunny	hot / sunny
November	hot / cloudy	cool / cloudy

1. (Tokyo / April) *What's the weather like in Tokyo in April?*

   It's usually cool and sunny.

2. (Buenos Aires / January) _____

   It's usually hot and rainy.

3. (Tokyo / August) _____

   It's usually hot and sunny.

4. What's the weather like in Buenos Aires in April?

   _____

5. What's the weather like in Tokyo in November?

   _____

2 Look at the pictures. Then write questions and answers.

1. **Q:** (What / see) *What can you see in the park?*

   A: You can see _____ in the park.

2. **Q:** (What / do) _____

   A: You can _____ at the beach.

3. **Q:** (see) _____

   A: Yes, you can. You can see a lot of

   _____ in the rain forest.

4. **Q:** (go camping) _____

   A: No, you can't. You can't

   _____ in the cave.

World of friends

1 Match the questions to the answers.

1. Who lives on a beautiful island? _d_

2. Who wants to learn German? _____

3. Who writes e-mail messages? _____

4. Who plays tennis? _____

5. Who watches French movies? _____

6. Who speaks Greek? _____

a. Kevin does. He writes to his e-pal every week!

b. Ashley and David do. They speak Italian, too.

c. I do! I watch American movies, too.

d. Yahaira does. She lives in Puerto Rico.

e. Frida does. She wants to visit Germany next year.

f. Sam and Mike do. They practice every day.

2 Write answers with *do* or *does*.

1. Who uses the Internet?

   (Tammy) _Tammy does._

2. Who speaks German?

   (Tina and Jan) _____

3. Who lives in Portugal?

   (Rodrigo) _____

4. Who plays soccer?

   (I) _____

5. Who lives in Morocco?

   (you) _____

6. Who speaks English?

   (we) _____

3 Look at the pictures. Then write questions and answers.

Buon Giorno!
Aldo

Ilana

Ingrid and Pamela

Tyler

Anton

Ahalan!
Dalia

1. **Q:** _Who speaks Arabic?_

   A: Dalia does.

2. **Q:** _____

   A: Tyler does.

3. **Q:** _____

   A: Ilana does.

4. **Q:** Who plays cards?

   A: _____

5. **Q:** Who skateboards?

   A: _____

6. **Q:** Who lives in Italy?

   A: _____

International Day

1 Write the numbers.

1. (589) _five hundred and eighty-nine_
2. (3,406) _____
3. (82,742) _____
4. (955,698) _____
5. (199) _____

6. (75,000) _____
7. (208,638) _____
8. (777) _____
9. (6,020) _____
10. (5,416) _____

2 Write questions and answers.

1. **Q:** (sports / you / like) _What sports do you like?_____

   A: (baseball / basketball) _I like baseball and basketball.____

2. **Q:** (languages / your father / speak) _____

   A: (English / German) _____

3. **Q:** (instruments / they / play) _____

   A: (piano / guitar) _____

4. **Q:** (animals / your mother / like) _____

   A: (cats / dogs) _____

5. **Q:** (desserts / you / eat) _____

   A: (ice cream / cake / cookies) _____

6. **Q:** (subjects / you / like) _____

   A: (English / science / math) _____

3 Answer the questions with your own information.

1. What animals do you like?
   _I like dogs and horses._____

2. What languages do you speak?

   _____

3. What subjects do you like?

   _____

4. What foods do you eat?

   _____

5. What sports do you play?

   _____

6. What movies do you watch?

   _____

1 **Read the article quickly. Is the weather around the world warmer now?**

Glacier National Park

Glacier National Park in the state of Montana in the United States is a very beautiful place. The park has many mountains, forests, and rivers. There are 26 glaciers in the park. A glacier is a very big area of ice. Some people say a glacier is like a river of ice.

There are a lot of animals in the park, like bears, wolves, and wild cats. But there aren't many snakes. They don't like the cold weather.

Visitors to the park need clothes for all kinds of weather, even in July and August. It sometimes snows in August! In one day, it can be very warm in the morning or afternoon and then very cold at night. But the park has a problem with the weather.

The weather around the world is warmer now. Why is this a problem? The glaciers are melting and some of the plants and animals are dying. Does Glacier National Park need a new name? Not now, but maybe some day!

2 **Check (✓) the correct words to complete the sentences.**

1. The ice in my tea is ☑ melting. ☐ dying.

2. It's sunny and ☐ cold ☐ warm today. You don't need a jacket.

3. Let's go hiking in the ☐ mountains. ☐ rivers.

4. Give that plant some water! It's ☐ melting. ☐ dying.

5. Many bears live in the ☐ river. ☐ forest.

3 **Read the article in Part 1 slowly. Are these sentences true or false? Write _T_ (true) or _F_ (false). Then correct the false sentences.**

1. Some people say a glacier is a river with a lot of water in it. _F_
   Some people say a glacier is like a river of ice.

2. There are a lot of snakes in Glacier National Park. _____

3. It never snows in August in Glacier National Park. _____

4. There's a problem with the melting ice in the park. _____

5. Some of the plants and animals in the park are dying. _____

A Complete the conversations with the questions in the box.

> ☐ Can you buy food at this hotel? ☐ What's the weather like in December?
> ☑ What can you see in this park? ☐ What's the weather like today?
> ☐ What movies do you like? ☐ Who hangs out at the mall after school?

1. **A** *What can you see in this park?*
   B You can see some incredible hot springs in this park.

2. **A** _____
   B It's warm and sunny today.

3. **A** _____
   B It's usually cold and snowy.

4. **A** _____
   B Marisol and Patricia do.

5. **A** _____
   B I like comedies and action movies.

6. **A** _____
   B Yes, you can.

B Look at the chart. Then write questions and answers about Liza and Eliot.

	Liza	**Eliot**
Sports	soccer, tennis	soccer, tennis
Movies	documentaries, dramas	action movies, comedies
Languages	English, German	English, German
Pets	dog, spiders	parrot

1. **Q:** (Eliot / watch) *What movies does Eliot watch?*
   A: *He watches action movies and comedies.*

2. **Q:** (Liza and Eliot / play) _____
   A: _____

3. **Q:** (Liza and Eliot / speak) _____
   A: _____

4. **Q:** (Liza / have) _____
   A: _____

Notes

Notes

Notes

Notes